D0206962

INTRODUCTION

In its issue for March 1898, *Harper's New Monthly Magazine* published Mark Twain's "Stirring Times in Austria," his eyewitness account of the outlandish parliamentary fracas that nearly spelled the end of the Austro-Hungarian Empire. Twain, who was traveling in Europe after the double blows of his bankruptcy and the death of his daughter Susy, took a calculatedly smug and superior view of European politics—one likely to appeal to his democratic Yankee readers back home.

As he took pains to point out, Austria-Hungary was "not a nation, but a collection of nations"—a fact reflected in the inhabitants of Vienna's grandiose Parliament House, which "draws its membership of 425 deputies from the nineteen or twenty states . . . who speak eleven languages. That means eleven distinct varieties of jealousies, hostilities, and warring interests. . . The Parliament is split up into many parties—the Clericals, the Progressists, the German Nationalists, the Young Czechs, the Social Democrats, the Christian Socialists, and some others—and it is difficult to get up working combinations among them. . . . As to the make-up of the House, . . . the deputies come from all walks of life and from all grades of society. There are princes, counts, barons, priests, peasants, mechanics, laborers, lawyers, judges, physicians, professors, merchants, bankers, shopkeepers. They are religious men; they are earnest, sincere, devoted; and they hate the Jews."

With France's Dreyfus Affair just coming to a boil, European anti-Semitism was so familiar to his readers that Twain felt it hardly worth mentioning, let alone exploring. He was more impressed by the fact that since 1867, the only thing holding Austria and Hungary together had been the *Ausgleich,* or Austro-Hungarian Compromise—a constitutional adjustment, arrangement, or settlement that, by law, had to be renewed every ten years.

In the closing days of 1897, Twain reported, "The ten-year rearrangement was due a year ago, but failed to connect—at least completely. A year's compromise was arranged. A new arrangement must be effected before the last day of this year. Otherwise, the two countries become separate entities."

But the Ausgleich was not the only item of pressing business before the Reichsrath, or Parliament. Count Badeni, who had formed a government in 1895, "could not carry on his government without a majority vote in the House. . . and in order to secure it, he had to make a trade of some sort. He made it with the Czechs—the Bohemians. The terms were not easy for him: He must pass a bill making the Czech tongue the official language in Bohemia in place of German.

"This created a storm. All the Germans in Austria were incensed. In numbers, they form but a fourth part of the Empire population, but they urge that the country's public business should be conducted in one common tongue, and that tongue a world language—which German is.

"However," Twain continued, "Badeni secured his majority. The German element in Parliament was apparently become helpless. The Czech deputies were exultant. Then the music began. . . .

Judy Konner

CONCERNING THE JEWS

Mark Twain

Running Press
Philadelphia, Pennsylvania

Copyright © 1985 by Running Press.
All rights reserved under the Pan-American
and International Copyright Conventions. This book may
not be reproduced in whole or in part in any form or by
any means electronic or mechanical, including
photocopying, recording, or by any information storage
and retrieval system now known or hereafter invented,
without written permission from the publisher.
Printed in the United States of America.
Canadian representatives: General Publishing,
30 Lesmill Road, Don Mills, Ontario M3B 2T6.
International representatives: Kaiman & Polon, Inc.,
2175 Lemoine Avenue, Fort Lee, New Jersey 07024.

9 8 7 6 5 4 3 2 1
Digit on the right indicates the number of this printing.

Library of Congress Cataloging in Publication Data
Twain, Mark, 1835-1910.
Concerning the Jews.
1. Antisemitism—Addresses, essays, lectures.
I. Title.
DS145.T9 1985 305.8'924 84-27665

ISBN: 0-89471-335-3 (Paper)
ISBN: 0-89471-336-1 (Library binding)

Cover design by Toby Schmidt
Editorial Consultant: Frank Freudberg
Cover illustration by Michael Schroeder
Typography: Garth by rci, Philadelphia, PA
Printed and bound by Port City Press, Baltimore, MD

This book can be ordered by mail from the
publisher. Please include 75¢ for postage.
But try your bookstore first.

Running Press
Book Publishers
125 South 22nd Street
Philadelphia, Pennsylvania 19103

"The government must get the Ausgleich through. It must not fail. Badeni's majority was ready to carry it through, but the [German] minority was determined to obstruct it and delay it until the obnoxious Czech-language measure should be shelved." The German opposition, then, had a good weapon to fight with: "If it could delay the Ausgleich a few weeks, the government would doubtless have to withdraw the hated language bill or lose Hungary."

Badeni's majority in the Reichsrath swiftly developed a strategy of its own: "It was the government's intention to push the Ausgleich through its preliminary stages in . . . one sitting (for which it was the Order to the Day) and then, by vote, refer it to a select committee." But the means of rushing those preliminary stages were, to Twain, startlingly crude: "It was the Majority's scheme—as charged by the [German] Opposition—to drown debate upon the bill by pure noise—drown it out and stop it. The debate being thus ended, the vote upon the reference would follow—with victory for the government.

"And now took place," Twain continued, "that memorable sitting of the House which . . . lasted the best part of two days and a night." At 8:45 P.M. on the night of October 28, 1897, Reichsrath President Ritter von Abrahamowicz, of Polish origin and "object of the [German] Opposition's limitless hatred," mounted the tribune and delivered himself of a single sentence: "Dr. Lecher has the floor."

Dr. Lecher was President of the Board of Trade in his native city of Brünn and was a staunch defender of the German language—as the Majority well knew. Thus it was that when Dr. Lecher rose to his feet, "then burst out another wild and frantic and deafening clamor as has not been heard on this planet since the last time the Comanches surprised a white settlement at midnight. Yells from the Left, counter-yells from the Right, explosions of yells from all sides at once; and all the air sawed and pawed and cloven by a writhing confusion of gesturing arms and hands. Out of the midst of this thunder and turmoil and tempest rose Dr. Lecher, serene and collected." He began his speech. "At any rate, his lips could be seen to be moving, and that was evidence."

At intervals, President Abrahamowicz "grasped his bell and swung it up and down with vigor, adding its keen clamor to the storm weltering down there below. Dr. Lecher went on with his pantomime speech, contented, untroubled. Here and there and now and then, powerful voices burst above the din and delivered an ejaculation that was heard. Then the din ceased for a moment or two, and gave opportunity to hear what the Chair might answer; then the noise broke out again. . . .

"WOLF *(hearable above the storm):* 'Mr. President, I demand the floor!' . . . The President blandly answered that Dr. Lecher had the floor. Which was true: and he was speaking, too, calmly, earnestly and argumentatively; and the official stenographers had left their places and were at his elbows taking down his words, he leaning and orating into their ears."

Later in the article, Twain added, "If I have reported the behavior of the House intelligibly, the reader. . . has probably supposed that the conduct exhibited at the Long Sitting was far out of the common, and due to special excitement and irritation . . . I will go back to a previous sitting in order to show that the deputies had already had some practice." Some of the deputies' customary remarks "were of a very candid sort," and Twain gave some examples, "not in their order, but selected on their merits:

". . . Wolf discharges a galling remark at Mr. Wohlmeyer.

"WOHLMEYER *(responding):* 'You Jew, you!'

"There is a moment's lull. . . . VIELOHLAWEK: 'I would rather take my hat off to a Jew than to Wolf!'

"STROHBACH *(To Wolf):* 'Jew-flunky! Here we have been fighting the Jews for ten years, and now you are helping them to power again. How much do you get for it?' "

Twain was as amazed by this rampant prejudice as by the extraordinarily personal insults hurled from deputy to deputy. As he laconically observed, "The difference between schoolboys and the law-makers of the Reichsrath seems to be that the law-makers have no limit, no danger-line. Apparently they may call each other what they please, and go home unmutilated."

On the night of October 28, however, it was quite clear to Twain what the imperturbable Dr. Lecher was up to by *not* responding to such taunts: "Into the government's calculations had not entered the possibility of a single-barreled speech which should occupy the entire time-limit of the sitting, and also get itself delivered in spite of all the noise. . . .

"There was but one way for Dr. Lecher to hold the floor—he must stay on his legs. If he should sit down to rest a moment, the floor would be taken from him by the enemy in the Chair." Dr. Lecher was, in effect, mounting a filibuster—but with an important difference: "In the English House, an obstructionist has held the floor with Bible readings and other outside matters, but Dr. Lecher could not have that restful and recuperative privilege—he must confine himself strictly to the subject before the House. More than once, when the President could not hear him because of the general tumult, he sent persons to listen and report as to whether the orator was speaking to the subject or not. . . .

"His speech was not formally prepared. He had a few notes jotted down for his guidance. He had his facts in his head, his heart was in his work, and for twelve hours he stood there, undisturbed by the clamor around him, and with grace and ease and confidence poured out the riches of his mind, in closely reasoned arguments" as to why the German Opposition wanted the Ausgleich to be amended before it was renewed.

"He was earning applause, and this enabled his party to turn that fact to account. Now and then they applauded him a couple of minutes on a stretch, and during that time he could stop speaking and rest his voice without having the floor taken from him. . . .

"When a man has been speaking eight hours, is it conceivable that he can still be interesting, still fascinating? When Dr. Lecher had been speaking eight hours, he was still compactly surrounded by friends who would not leave him and by foes (of all parties) who *could* not; and all hung enchanted and wondering upon his words, and all testified their admiration with constant and cordial outbursts of applause. . . .

"During the twelve-hour effort, friends brought to the orator three glasses of wine, four cups of coffee, and one glass of beer—a most stingy reinforcement of his wasting tissues, but the hostile Chair would permit no addition to it. But no matter, the Chair could not beat that man. He was a garrison holding a fort, and he was not to be starved out. . . .

"He finished his long speech in these terms, as nearly as a permissibly free translation can convey them: '. . . In any case, gentlemen of the Majority, make sure of this: Henceforth, as before, you will find us at our post. The Germans of Austria will neither surrender nor die!' Then burst a storm of applause which rose and fell, rose and fell, burst out again and again and again, explosion after explosion, hurricane after hurricane, with no apparent promise of ever coming to an end. . . .

"In consequence of Dr. Lecher's twelve-hour speech and the other obstructions furbished by the Minority, the famous thirty-three hour sitting of the House accomplished nothing. The government side had made a supreme effort. . . yet had failed to get the Ausgleich into the hands of a committee. This was a severe defeat. . . . Parliament was adjourned for a week, to let the members cool off, perhaps—a sacrifice of precious time, for but two months remained in which to carry the all-important Ausgleich to a consummation.

"During the month of November," Twain continued, "things went from bad to worse. The all-important Augsleich remained hard aground, and could not be sparred off. . . . On Thanksgiving Day, the sitting was a history-making one. On that day, the harried, bedeviled, and despairing government went insane. In order to free itself from the thraldom of the [German] Opposition, it. . . moved an important change in the Rules."

Once again, the government's tactics were extremely underhanded: "The usual storm was raging in the House. As usual, many of the Minority and the most of the Majority were standing up—to have a better chance to exchange epithets and make other noises. Into this storm Count Falkenhayn entered, with his paper in his hand; and all at once there was a rush to get near him and hear him read his motion."

When Falkenhayn took his seat again, President Abrahamowicz immediately forbade debate upon the Count's motion and put it to a stand-up vote instead of yeas and nays: "Persons desiring to vote in the affirmative, *stand up!*"

"The House was already standing up," Twain remarked, "and before a third of it had found out what the President had been saying, he had proclaimed the adoption of the motion! . . . The 'Lex Falkenhayn,' thus strangely born, gave the President power to suspend for three days any deputy who should continue to be disorderly after being called to order twice. . . . On these terms, the Ausgleich could be put through in an hour—apparently!"

During the next day's session, however, "the customary storm of noises burst out, and rose higher and higher, and wilder and wilder, and really seemed to surpass anything that had gone before it in that place. The President took his seat and begged for order, but no one could hear him."

Below him in the crowd, some two dozen Socialists were scowling up at him, roaring insults and shaking their fists at him. After a few minutes of this, the Socialists all at once "stormed up through the ministerial benches . . . snatched the documents that lay on the President's desk and flung them abroad. . . . Meantime, a detail of Socialists had swarmed up the side steps and overflowed the President and Vice and were crowding and shouldering and shoving them out of the place," down the steps, and across the House. "One could see fists go up and come down, with other signs and shows of a heady fight. Then the President and the Vice disappeared through the door of the entrance; and the victorious Socialists turned and marched back, mounted the tribune, flung the President's bell and remaining papers abroad . . . and held the place as if it were a fortress. Their friends on the floor were in a frenzy of triumph, and manifested it in a deafening way. The whole House was on its feet, amazed and wondering."

They did not have long to wonder. The door opened again, and in came "a uniformed and helmeted battalion of bronzed and stalwart men marching in double file down the floor of the House. . . . These sixty policemen had been soldiers, and they went at their work with the cold unsentimentality of their trade. They ascended the steps of the tribune, laid their hands upon the inviolable persons of the representatives of a nation, and dragged and tugged and hauled them down the steps and out at the door. . . .

"Some of the results of this wild freak followed instantly," Twain concluded. "The Badeni government came down with a crash. There was a popular outbreak or two in Vienna. There were three or four days of furious rioting in Prague, followed by the establishing there of martial law. The Jews and Germans were harried and plundered, and their houses destroyed. In other Bohemian towns there was rioting—in some cases the Germans being the rioters, in others the Czechs—and in all cases, the Jew had to roast, no matter which side he was on."

Twain firmly believed that the entry of the police into the Reichsrath had been "a tremendous episode. The memory of it will outlast all the thrones that exist today. . . . It takes its imposing place among the world's unforgettable things." And clearly he counted on the deputies' outrageous behavior to astonish and amuse his American readers: "We imagine that we are back fifty years ago in the Arkansas Legislature, and we think we know what is going to happen, and we are glad we came, and glad we are up in the gallery, out of the way, where we can see the whole thing and yet not to have to supply any material for the inquest." Yet it was his almost matter-of-fact references to prejudice and persecution that prompted the most response from the readers of *Harper's*—as Twain himself endeavored to explain in the September 1898 issue, by way of a follow-up article entitled "Concerning the Jews."

CONCERNING THE JEWS

Some months ago I published a magazine article descriptive of a remarkable scene in the Imperial Parliament in Vienna. Since then, I have received from Jews in America several letters of inquiry. They were difficult letters to answer, for they were not very definite. But at last I have received a definite one. It is from a lawyer, and he really asks the questions which the other writers probably believed they were asking. By help of this text I will do the best I can to publicly answer this correspondent, and also the others—at the same time apologizing for having failed to reply privately.

The lawyer's letter reads as follows:

> *I have read "Stirring Times in Austria." One point in particular is of vital import to not a few thousand people, including myself, being a point about which I have often wanted to address a question to some disinterested person. The show of military force in the Austrian Parliament, which precipitated the riots, was not introduced by any Jew. No Jew was a member of that*

body. No Jewish question was involved in the Ausgleich *or in the language proposition. No Jew was insulting anybody. In short, no Jew was doing any mischief toward anybody whatsoever. In fact the Jews were the only ones of the nineteen different races in Austria which did not have a party—they are absolutely non-participants. Yet in your article, you say that in the rioting which followed, all classes of people were unanimous only on one thing:* viz., *in being against the Jews.*

Now will you kindly tell me why, in your judgment, the Jews have thus ever been and are even now, in these days of supposed intelligence, the butt of baseless, vicious animosities? I dare say that for centuries there have been no more quiet, undisturbing, and well-behaving citizens, as a class, than that same Jew. It seems to me that ignorance and fanaticism cannot alone account for these horrible and unjust persecutions.

Tell me, therefore, from your vantage point of cold view, what in your mind is the cause. Can American Jews do anything to correct it either in America or abroad? Will it ever come to an end? Will a Jew be permitted to live honestly, decently, and peaceably like the rest of mankind? What has become of the Golden Rule?

I will begin by saying that if I thought myself prejudiced against the Jew, I should hold it fairest to leave this subject to a person not crippled in that way. But I think I have no such prejudice. A few years ago, a Jew observed to me that there was no uncourteous reference to his people in my books and asked how it happened. It happened because the disposition was lacking. I am quite sure that (bar one) I have no race prejudices and I think I have no color prejudices, nor caste prejudices, nor creed prejudices. Indeed, I know it. I can stand any society. All that I care to know is that a man is a human being—that is enough for me: he can't be any worse.

I have no special regard for Satan, but I can at least claim I have no prejudice against him. It may even be that I lean a little his way, on account of his not having a fair show. All religions issue bibles against him and say the most injurious things about him, but we never hear *his* side. We have none but the evidence for the prosecution, and yet we have rendered the verdict. To my mind, this is irregular. It is un-English; it is un-American; it *is* French. Without this precedent, Dreyfus could not have been condemned.

Of course Satan has some kind of a case, it goes without saying. It may be a poor one, but that is nothing; that can be said about any of us. As soon as I can get at the facts, I will undertake his rehabilitation myself, if I can find an unpolitic publisher. It is a thing which we ought to be willing to do for anyone who is under a cloud. We may not pay him reverence, for that would be indiscreet, but we can at least respect his talents. A person who has for untold centuries maintained the imposing position of spiritual head of four-fifths of the human race, and political head of the whole of it, must be granted the possession of executive abilities of the loftiest order. In his large presence, the other popes and politicians shrink to midges for the microscope. I would like to see him. I would rather see him and shake him by the tail than any other member of the European Concert.

In the present paper, I shall allow myself to use the word "Jew" as if it stood for both religion and race. It is handy; and besides, that is what the term means to the general world.

In the above letter, one notes these points:

1. The Jew is a well-behaved citizen.
2. Can ignorance and fanaticism *alone* account for his unjust treatment?
3. Can Jews do anything to improve the situation?
4. The Jews have no party; they are non-participants.
5. Will the persecution ever come to an end?
6. What has become of the Golden Rule?

Point No. 1—We must grant Proposition No. 1, for several sufficient reasons. The Jew is not a disturber of the peace of any country. Even his enemies will concede that. He is not a loafer, he is not a sot, he is not noisy, he is not a brawler nor a rioter, he is not quarrelsome. In the statistics of crime, his presence is conspicuously rare—in all countries. With murder and other crimes of violence he has but little to do: he is a stranger to the hangman. In the police court's daily long roll of "assaults" and "drunk and disorderlies," his name seldom appears.

That the Jewish home is a home in the truest sense is a fact which no one will dispute. The family is knitted together by the strongest affections; its members show each other every due respect; and reverence for the elders is an inviolate law of the house.

The Jew is not a burden on the charities of the state nor of the city; these could cease from their functions without affecting him. When he is well enough, he works; when he is incapacitated, his own people take care of him—and not in a poor and stingy way, but with a fine and large benevolence. His race is entitled to be called the most benevolent of all the races of men. A Jewish beggar is not impossible, perhaps: such a thing may exist, but there are few men that can say they have seen that spectacle. The Jew has been staged in many uncomplimentary forms, but so far as I know, no dramatist has done him the injustice to stage him as a beggar. Whenever a Jew has real need to beg, his people save him from the necessity of doing it. The charitable institutions of the Jews are supported by Jewish money, and amply. The Jews make no noise about it; it is done quietly; they do not nag and pester and harass us for contributions; they give us peace and set us an example—an example which we have not found ourselves able to follow; for by nature we are not free givers and have to be patiently and persistently hunted down in the interest of the unfortunate.

These facts are all on the credit side of the proposition that the Jew is a good and orderly citizen. Summed up, they certify that he is quiet, peaceable, industrious, unaddicted to high crimes and brutal dispositions; that his family life is commendable; that he is not a burden upon public charities; that he is not a beggar; that in benevolence he is above the reach of competition. These are the very quintessentials of good citizenship. If you can add that he is as honest as the average of his neighbors—but I think that question is affirmatively answered by the fact that he is a successful businessman. The basis of successful business is honesty; a business cannot thrive where the parties to it cannot trust each other. In the matter of numbers, the Jew counts for little in the overwhelming population of New York, but that his honesty counts for much is guaranteed by the fact that the immense wholesale business of Broadway, from the Battery to Union Square, is substantially in his hands.

I suppose that the most picturesque example in history of a trader's trust in his fellow-trader was one where it was not Christian trusting Christian, but Christian trusting Jew. That Hessian Duke who used to sell his subjects to George III to fight George Washington with got rich at it; and by-and-by, when the wars engendered by the French Revolution made his throne too warm for him, he was obliged to fly the country. He was in a hurry and had to leave his earnings behind—$9,000,000. He had to risk the money with someone without security. He did not select a Christian, but a Jew—a Jew of only modest means, but of high character; a character so high it left him lonesome: Rothschild of Frankfort. Thirty years later, when Europe had become quiet and safe again, the Duke came back from overseas, and the Jew returned the loan, with interest added.

Here is another piece of picturesque history, and it reminds us that shabbiness and dishonesty are not the monopoly of any race or creed, but are merely human:

> *Congress has passed a bill to pay $379.56 to Moses Pendergrass, of Libertyville, Missouri. The story of the reason of this liberality is pathetically interesting and shows the sort of pickle that an honest man may get into who undertakes to do an honest job of work for Uncle Sam. In 1886, Moses Pendergrass put in a bid for the contract to carry the mail on the route from Knob Lick to Libertyville and Coffman, thirty miles a day, from July 1, 1887, for one year. He got the postmaster at Knob Lick to write the letter for him, and while Moses intended that his bid should be $400, his scribe carelessly made it $4.*
>
> *Moses got the contract and did not find out about the mistake until the end of the first quarter, when he got his first pay. When he found out at what rate he was working, he was sorely cast down and opened communication with the Post Office Department. The Department informed him that he must either carry out his contract or throw it up; and that if he threw it up, his*

> *bondsman would have to pay the government $1,459.85 damages. So Moses carried out his contract, walked thirty miles every weekday for a year, and carried the mail, and received for his labor $4—or to be accurate, $6.84, for, the route being extended after his bid was accepted, the pay was proportionately increased. Now, after ten years, a bill was finally passed to pay to Moses the difference between what he earned in that unlucky year and what he received.*

The *Sun,* which tells the above story, says that bills were introduced in three or four Congresses for Moses's relief, and that committees repeatedly investigated his claim.

It took six Congresses, containing in their persons the compressed virtues of 70,000,000 of people, and cautiously and carefully giving expression to those virtues in the fear of God and the next election, eleven years to find out some way to cheat a fellow-Christian out of about $13 on his honestly executed contract and out of nearly $300 due him on its enlarged terms. And they succeeded. During the same time, they paid out nearly $1,000,000,000 in pensions—a third of it unearned and undeserved. This indicates a splendid all-around competency in theft, for it starts with farthings and works its industries all the way up to shiploads. It may be possible that the Jews can beat this, but the man that bets on it is taking chances.

The Jew has his other side. He has some discreditable ways, though he has not a monopoly on them, because he cannot get entirely rid of vexatious Christian competition. We have seen that he seldom transgresses the laws against crimes of violence. Indeed, his dealings with courts are almost restricted to matters connected with commerce. He has a reputation for various small forms of cheating, and for practicing oppressive usury, and for burning himself out to get the insurance, and for arranging contracts which leave him an exit but lock the other man in, and for smart evasions which find him safe and comfortable just within the strict letter of the law, when court and jury know very well that he has violated the spirit of it. He is a frequent and faithful and capable officer in the civil service, but he is charged with an unpatriotic disinclination to stand by the flag as a soldier—like the Christian Quaker.

Now, if you offset these discreditable features by the creditable ones summarized in a preceding paragraph beginning with the words, "These facts are all on the credit side," and strike a balance, what must the verdict be? This, I think: that, the merits and demerits being fairly weighed and measured on both sides, the Christian can claim no superiority over the Jew in the matter of good citizenship.

Yet in all countries, from the dawn of history, the Jew has been persistently and implacably hated, and with frequency persecuted.

Point No. 2—"Can fanaticism *alone* account for this?" Years ago, I used to think that it was responsible for nearly all of it, but latterly I have come to think that this was an error. Indeed, it is now my conviction that it is responsible for hardly any of it.

In this connection, I call to mind Genesis, Chapter XLVII. We have all thoughtfully—or *un*thoughtfully—read the pathetic story of the years of plenty and the years of famine in Egypt; and how Joseph, with that opportunity, made a corner in broken hearts, and the crusts of the poor, and human liberty—a corner whereby he took a nation's money all away, to the last penny; took a nation's livestock all away, to the last hoof; took a nation's land away, to the last acre; then took the nation itself, buying it for bread, man by man, woman by woman, child by child, till all were slaves; a corner which took everything, left nothing; a corner so stupendous that by comparison with it, the most gigantic corners in subsequent history are but baby things, for it dealt in hundreds of millions of bushels, and its profits were reckonable by hundreds of millions of dollars, and it was a disaster so crushing that its effects have not wholly disappeared from Egypt today, more than three thousand years after the event.

Is it presumable that the eye of Egypt was upon Joseph, the foreign Jew, all this time? I think it likely. Was it friendly? We must doubt it. Was Joseph establishing a character for his race which would survive long in Egypt? And in time, would his name come to be familiarly used to express that character—like Shylock's? It is hardly to be doubted. Let us remember that this was *centuries before the Crucifixion.*

I wish to come down eighteen hundred years later and refer to a remark made by one of the Latin historians. I read it in a translation many years ago, and it comes back to me now with force. It was alluding to a time when people were still living who could have seen the Savior in the flesh. Christianity was so new that the people of Rome had hardly heard of it, and had but confused notions of what it was. The substance of the remark was this: Some Christians were persecuted in Rome through error, they being *"mistaken for Jews."*

The meaning seems plain. These pagans had nothing against Christians, but they were quite ready to persecute Jews. For some reason or other, they hated a Jew before they even knew what a Christian was. May I not assume, then, that the persecution of Jews is a thing which *antedates* Christianity and not born of Christianity? I think so. What was the origin of that feeling?

When I was a boy in the back settlements of the Mississippi Valley where a gracious and beautiful Sunday-school simplicity and unpracticality prevailed, the "Yankee" (citizen of the New England states) was hated with a splendid energy. But religion had nothing to do with it. In a trade, the Yankee was held to be about five times the match of the Westerner. His shrewdness, his insight, his judgment, his knowledge, his enterprise, and his formidable cleverness in applying these forces were frankly confessed, and most competently cursed.

In the Cotton States, after the war, the simple and ignorant Negroes made the crops for the white planter on shares. The Jew came down in force, set up shop on the plantation, supplied all the Negro's wants on credit, and at the end of the season was proprietor of the Negro's share of the present crop and of part of the share of his next one. Before long, the whites detested the Jew, and it is doubtful if the Negro loved him.

The Jew is being legislated out of Russia. The reason is not concealed. The movement was instituted because the Christian peasant and villager stood no chance against his commercial abilities. He was always ready to lend money on a crop and sell vodka and other necessaries of life on credit while the crop was growing. When settlement day came, he owned the crop; and next year or year after, he owned the farm, like Joseph.

In the dull and ignorant England of John's time, everybody got into debt to the Jew. He gathered all lucrative enterprises into his hands; he was the king of commerce; he was ready to be helpful in all profitable ways; he even financed crusades for the rescue of the Sepulchre. To wipe out his account with the nation and restore business to its natural and incompetent channels, he had to be banished from the realm.

For the like reasons, Spain had to banish him four hundred years ago, and Austria about a couple of centuries later. In all the ages, Christian Europe has been obliged to curtail his activities. If he entered upon a mechanical trade, the Christian had to retire from it. If he set up as a doctor, he was the best one and he took the business. If he exploited agriculture, the other farmers had to get at something else. Since there was no way to successfully compete with him in any vocation, the law had to step in and save the Christian from the poorhouse. Trade after trade was taken away from the Jew by statute till practically none was left. He was forbidden to engage in agriculture; he was forbidden to practice law; he was forbidden to practice medicine, except among Jews; he was forbidden the handicrafts. Even the seats of learning and the schools of science had to be closed against this tremendous antagonist.

Still, almost bereft of employments, he found ways to make money, even ways to get rich—also ways to invest his takings well, for usury was not denied him. In the hard conditions suggested, the Jew without brains could not survive, and the Jew with brains had to keep them in good training and well sharpened up, or starve. Ages of restriction to the one tool which the law was not able to take from—his brain—have made that tool singularly competent; ages of compulsory disuse of his hands have atrophied them, and he never uses them now. This history has a very, very commercial look, a most sordid and practical commercial look, the business aspect of a Chinese cheap-labor crusade. Religious prejudices may account for one part of it, but not for the other nine.

Protestants have persecuted Catholics, but they did not take their livelihoods away from them. The Catholics have persecuted the Protestants with bloody and awful bitterness, but they never closed agriculture and the handicrafts against them. Why was that? That has the candid look of genuine religious persecution, and not a trade-union boycott in a religious disguise.

The Jews are harried and obstructed in Austria and Germany, and lately in France; but England and America give them an open field and yet survive. Scotland offers them an unembarrassed field too, but there are not many takers. There are a few Jews in Glasgow, and one in Aberdeen, but that is because they can't earn enough to get away. The Scotch pay themselves that compliment, but it is authentic.

I feel convinced that the Crucifixion has not much to do with the world's attitude toward the Jew; that the reasons for it are older than that event, as suggested by Egypt's experience and by Rome's regret for having persecuted an unknown quantity called a Christian, under the mistaken impression that she was merely persecuting a Jew. *Merely* a Jew—a skinned eel who was used to it, presumably. I am persuaded that in Russia, Austria, and Germany, nine-tenths of the hostility toward the Jew comes from the average Christian's inability to compete successfully with the Jew in business—in either straight business or the questionable sort.

In Berlin a few years ago, I read a speech which frankly urged the expulsion of the Jews from Germany; and the agitator's *reason* was as frank as his proposition. It was this: that *eighty-five percent* of the successful lawyers of Berlin were Jews, and that about the same percentage of the great and lucrative businesses of all sorts in Germany were in the hands of the Jewish race! Isn't it an amazing confession? It was but another way of saying that in a population of 48,000,000, of whom only

500,000 were registered as Jews, eighty-five percent of the brains and honesty of the whole was lodged in the Jews. I must insist upon the honesty—it is an essential of successful business, taken by and large. Of course it does not rule out rascals entirely, even among Christians, but it is a good working rule nevertheless. The speaker's figures may have been inexact, but *the motive of persecution* stands out as clear as day.

The man claimed that in Berlin, the banks, the newspapers, the theaters, the great mercantile, shipping, mining, and manufacturing interests, the big army and city contracts, the tramways, and pretty much all other properties of high value—and *also* the small businesses—were in the hands of the Jews. He said the Jew was pushing the Christian to the wall all along the line; that it was all a Christian could do to scrape together a living; and that the Jew *must* be banished, and soon—there was no other way of saving the Christian. Here in Vienna last autumn, an agitator said that all these disastrous details were true of Austria-Hungary also; and in fierce language he demanded the expulsion of the Jews. When politicians come out without a blush and read the baby act in this frank way, *unrebuked,* it is a very good indication that they have a market back of them and know where to fish for votes.

You note the crucial point of the mentioned agitation: the argument is that the Christian cannot *compete* with the Jew, and that hence his very bread is in peril. To human beings, this is a much more hate-inspiring thing than is any detail connected with religion. With most people, of a necessity, bread and meat take first rank, religion second. I am convinced that the persecution of the Jew is not due in any large degree to religious prejudice.

No, the Jew is a money-getter; and in getting his money, he is a very serious obstruction to less capable neighbors who are on the same quest. I think that that is the trouble. In estimating worldly values, the Jew is not shallow, but deep. With precocious wisdom, he found out in the morning of time that some men worship rank, some worship heroes, some worship power, some worship God, and that over these ideals they dispute and cannot unite—but that they all worship money; so he made it the end and aim of his life to get it. He was at it in Egypt thirty-six centuries ago; he was at it in Rome when that Christian got persecuted by mistake for him; he has been at it ever since. The cost to him has been heavy; his success has made the whole human race his enemy—but it has paid, for it has brought him envy, and that is the only thing which men will sell both body and soul to get. He long ago observed that a millionaire commands respect, a two-millionaire homage, a multi-millionaire the deepest deeps of adoration. We all know that feeling; we have seen it express itself. We have noticed that when the average man mentions the name of a multi-millionaire, he does it with that mixture in his voice of awe and reverence and lust which burns in a Frenchman's eye when it falls on another man's centime.

Point No. 4.—"The Jews have no party; they are non-participants."

Perhaps you have let the secret out and given yourself away. It seems hardly a credit to the race that it is able to say that; or to you, sir, that you can say it without remorse; more, that you should offer it as a plea against maltreatment, injustice, and oppression. Who gives the Jew the right; who gives any race the right, to sit still in a free country and let somebody else look after its safety?

The oppressed Jew was entitled to all pity in the former times under brutal aristocracies, for he was weak and friendless and had no way to help his case. But he has ways now, and he has had them for a century, but I do not see that he has tried to make serious use of them. When the Revolution set him free in France, it was an act of grace—the grace of other people; he does not appear in it as a helper. I do not know that he helped when England set him free. Among the Twelve Sane Men of France who have stepped forward with great Zola at their head to fight (and win, I hope and believe) the battle for the most infamously misused Jew of modern times, do you find a great or rich or illustrious Jew helping? In the United States, he was created free in the beginning—he did not need to help, of course. In Austria and Germany and France he has a vote, but of what considerable use is it to him? He doesn't seem to know how to apply it to the best effect. With all his splendid capacities and all his fat wealth, he is today not politically important in any country.

In America, as early as 1854, the ignorant Irish hod-carrier, who had a spirit of his own and a way of exposing it to the weather, made it apparent to all that he must be politically reckoned with; yet fifteen years before that, we hardly knew what an Irishman looked like. As an intelligent force, and numerically, he has always been away down, but he has governed the country just the same. It was because he was *organized.* It made his vote valuable—in fact, essential.

You will say that the Jew is everywhere numerically feeble. That is nothing to the point—with the Irishman's history as an object lesson. But I am coming to your numerical feebleness presently. In all parliamentary countries, you could no doubt elect Jews to the legislatures—and even *one* member in such a body is sometimes a force which counts. How deeply have you concerned yourselves about this in Austria, France, and Germany? Or even in America, for that matter? You remark that the Jews were not to blame for the riots in this Reichsrath here, and you add with satisfaction that there wasn't one in that body. That is not strictly correct; if it were, would it not be in order for you to explain it and apologize for it, not to try to make a merit of it? But I think that the Jew was by no means in as large force there as he ought to have been, with his chances. Austria opens the suffrage to him on fairly liberal terms, and it must surely be his own fault that he is so much in the background politically.

As to your numerical weakness, I mentioned some figures a while ago—500,000—as the Jewish population of Germany. I will add some more: 6,000,000 in Russia, 5,000,000 in Austria, 250,000 in the United States. I take them from memory; I read them in the *Cyclopaedia Britannica* ten or twelve years ago. Still, I am entirely sure of them. If those statistics are correct, my argument is not as strong as it ought to be as concerns America, but it still has strength. It is plenty strong enough as concerns Austria, for ten years ago, 5,000,000 was nine percent of the empire's population. The Irish would govern the Kingdom of Heaven if they had a strength there like that.

I have some suspicions; I got them at second hand, but they have remained with me these ten or twelve years. When I read in the *C.B.* that the Jewish population of the United States was 250,000, I wrote the editor and explained to him that I was personally acquainted with more Jews than that in my country, and that his figures were without a doubt a misprint for 25,000,000. I also added that I was personally acquainted with *that* many there; but that was only to raise his confidence in me, for it was not true.

His answer miscarried, and I never got it; but I went around talking about the matter, and people told me they had reason to suspect that for business reasons, many Jews whose dealings were mainly with the Christians did not report themselves as Jews in the census. It looked plausible; it looks plausible yet. Look at the city of New York; and look at Boston and Philadelphia and New Orleans and Chicago and Cincinnati and San Francisco—how your race swarms in those places!—and everywhere else in America, down to the least little village. Read the signs on the marts of commerce and on the shops: Goldstein (gold stone), Edelstein (precious stone), Blumenthal (flower-vale), Rosenthal (rose-vale), Veilchenduft (violet odor), Singvogel (songbird), Rosenzweig (rose branch), and all the amazing list of beautiful and enviable names which Prussia and Austria glorified you with so long ago. It is another instance of Europe's coarse and cruel persecution of your race; not that it was coarse and cruel to outfit it with pretty and poetical names like those, but that it was coarse and cruel to make it *pay* for them or else take such hideous and often indecent names that today their owners never use them; or, if they do, only on official papers. And it was the many, not the few, who got the odious names, they being too poor to bribe the officials to grant them better ones.

Now, why was the race renamed? I have been told that in Prussia, it was given to using fictitious names and often changing them, so as to beat the tax-gatherer, escape military service, and so on; and that finally the idea was hit upon of furnishing all the inmates of a house with *one and the same surname* and then holding the house responsible right along for those inmates, and accountable for any disappearances that might occur; it made the Jews keep track of *each other* for self-interest's sake and spared the government the trouble.

In Austria, the renaming was merely done because the Jews in some newly acquired regions had no surnames, but were mostly named Abraham and Moses; and therefore the tax-gatherer could not tell t'other from which and was likely to lose his reason over the matter. The renaming was put into the hands of the War Department, and a charming mess the graceless young lieutenants made of it. To them, a Jew was of no sort of consequence, and they labelled the race in a way to make the angels weep. As an example, take these two: Abraham Bellyache and Schmul Godbedamned—culled from *Namens Studien* by Karl Emil Franzos.

If that explanation of how the Jews of Prussia came to be renamed is correct; if it is true that they fictitiously registered themselves to gain certain advantages, it may possibly be true that in America they refrain from registering themselves as Jews to fend off the damaging prejudices of the Christian customer. I have no way of knowing whether this notion is well-founded or not. There may be other and better ways of explaining why only that poor little 250,000 of our Jews got into the *Cyclopaedia.* I may, of course, be mistaken, but I am strongly of the opinion that we have an immense Jewish population in America.

Point No. 3—"Can Jews do anything to improve the situation?"

I think so. If I may make a suggestion without seeming to be trying to teach my grandmother how to suck eggs, I will offer it. In our days, we have learned the value of combination. We apply it everywhere—in railway systems, in trusts, in trade unions, in

Salvation Armies, in minor politics, in major politics, in European Concerts. Whatever our strength may be, big or little, we *organize* it. We have found out that that is the only way to get the most out of it that is in it. We know the weakness of individual sticks, and the strength of the concentrated fagot. Suppose you try a scheme like this, for instance: In England and America, put every Jew on the census-book *as* a Jew (in case you have not been doing that). Get up volunteer regiments composed of Jews solely and, when the drum beats, fall in and go to the front, so as to remove the reproach that you have few Massenas among you, and that you feed on a country but don't like to fight for it.

Next, in politics, organize your strength, band together, and deliver the casting vote where you can; and where you can't, compel as good terms as possible. You huddle to yourselves already in all countries, but you huddle to no sufficient purpose, politically speaking. You do not seem to be organized, except for your charities. There you are omnipotent; there you compel your due of recognition—you do not have to beg for it. It shows what you can do when you band together for a definite purpose.

And then from America and England you can encourage your race in Austria, France, and Germany, and materially help it. It was a pathetic tale that was told by a poor Jew in Galicia a fortnight ago during the riots, after he had been raided by the Christian peasantry and despoiled of everything he had. He said his vote was of no value to him, and he wished he could be excused from casting it, for indeed, casting it was a sure *damage* to him, since no matter which party he voted for, the other party would come straight and take its revenge out of him. Nine percent of the population of the empire, these Jews, and apparently they cannot put a plank into any candidate's platform! If you will send our Irish lads over here, I think they will organize your race and change the aspect of the Reichsrath.

You seem to think that the Jews take no hand in politics here, that they are "absolutely non-participants." I am assured by men competent to speak that this is a very large error, that the Jews are exceedingly active in politics all over the empire, but that they scatter their work and their votes among the numerous parties and thus lose the advantages to be had by concentration. I think that in America they scatter too, but you know more about that than I do.

Speaking of concentration, Dr. Herzl has a clear insight into the value of that. Have you heard of his plan? He wishes to gather the Jews of the world together in Palestine, with a government of their own—under the suzerainty of the Sultan, I suppose. At the convention of Berne last year, there were delegates from everywhere, and the proposal was received with decided favor. I am not the Sultan, and I am not objecting; but if that concentration of the cunningest brains in the world was going to be made in a free country (bar Scotland), I think it would be politic to stop it. It will not be well to let that race find out its strength. If the horses knew theirs, we should not ride any more.

Point No. 5—"Will the persecution of the Jews ever come to an end?"

On the score of religion, I think it has already come to an end. On the score of race prejudice and trade, I have the idea that it will continue—that is, here and there in spots about the world, where a barbarous ignorance and a sort of mere animal civilization prevail; but I do not think that elsewhere the Jew need now stand in any fear of being robbed and raided. Among the high civilizations, he seems to be very comfortably situated indeed, and to have more than his proportionate share of the prosperities going. It has that look in Vienna. I suppose the race prejudice cannot be removed; but he can stand that: it is no particular matter. By his make and ways, he is substantially a foreigner wherever he may be, and even the angels dislike a foreigner.

I am using this word "foreigner" in the German sense—*stranger.* Nearly all of us have an antipathy to a stranger, even of our own nationality. We pile gripsacks in a vacant seat to keep him from getting it; and a dog goes further and does as a savage would—challenges him on the spot. The German dictionary seems to make no distinction between a stranger and a foreigner; in its view, a stranger *is* a foreigner—a sound position, I think. You will always be by ways and habits and predilections substantially strangers—foreigners—wherever you are, and that will probably keep the race prejudice against you alive.

But you were the favorites of Heaven originally, and your manifold and unfair prosperities convince me that you have crowded back into that snug place again. Here is an incident that is significant. Last week in Vienna, a hailstorm struck the prodigious Central Cemetery and made wasteful destruction there. In the Christian part of it, according to the official figures, 621 windowpanes were broken, more than 900 singing-birds were killed, five great trees and many small ones were torn to shreds and the shreds scattered far and wide by the wind, the ornamental plants and other decorations of the graves were ruined, and more than a hundred tomb lanterns shattered; and it took the cemetery's whole force of 300 laborers more than three days to clear away the storm's wreckage. In the report occurs this remark—and in its italics, you can hear it grit its Christian teeth: "... lediglich die *israelitische* Abtheilung des Friedhofes vom Hagelwetter *ganzlich verschont* worden war." Not a hailstone hit the Jewish reservation! Such nepotism makes me tired.

Point No. 6—"What has become of the Golden Rule?"

It exists, it continues to sparkle, and is well taken care of. It is Exhibit A in the Church's assets, and we pull it out every Sunday and give it an airing. But you are not permitted to try to smuggle it into this discussion, where it is irrelevant and would not feel at home. It is strictly religious furniture, like an acolyte or a contribution plate, or any of those things. It has never been intruded into business; and Jewish persecution is not a religious passion, it is a business passion.

To conclude.—If the statistics are right, the Jews constitute but *one percent* of the human race. It suggests a nebulous dim puff of stardust lost in the blaze of the Milky Way. Properly, the Jew ought hardly to be heard of, but he is heard of, has always been heard of. He is as prominent on the planet as any other people, and his commercial importance is extravagantly out of proportion to the smallness of his bulk. His contributions to the world's list of great names in literature, science, art, music, finance, medicine, and abstruse learning are also away out of proportion to the weakness of his numbers. He has made a marvellous fight in this world, in all the ages; and has done it with his hands tied behind him. He could be vain of himself, and be excused for it. The Egyptian, the Babylonian, and the Persian rose, filled the planet with sound and splendor, then faded to dream stuff and passed away. The Greek and the Roman followed, and made a vast noise, and they are gone. Other peoples have sprung up and held their torch high for a time, but it burned out, and they sit in twilight now, or have vanished. The Jew saw them all, beat them all, and is now what he always was, exhibiting no decadence, no infirmities of age, no weakening of his parts, no slowing of his energies, no dulling of his alert and aggressive mind. All things are mortal but the Jew; all other forces pass, but he remains. What is the secret of his immortality?

Postscript: The Jew as Soldier

When I published the above article in *Harper's Monthly,* I was ignorant—like the rest of the Christian world—of the fact that the Jew had a record as a soldier. I have since seen the official statistics, and I find that he furnished soldiers and high officers to the Revolution, the War of 1812, and the Mexican War. In the Civil War, he was represented in the armies and navies of both the North and the South by ten percent of his numerical strength—the same percentage that was furnished by the Christian population of the two sections.

This large fact means more than it seems to mean, for it means that the Jew's patriotism was not merely level with the Christian's, but overpassed it. When the Christian volunteer arrived in camp, he got a welcome and applause, but as a rule, the Jew got a snub. His company was not desired, and he was made to feel it. That he nevertheless conquered his wounded pride and sacrificed both that and his blood for his flag raises the average and quality of his patriotism above the Christian's. His record for capacity, for fidelity, and for gallant soldiership in the field is as good as anyone's. This is true of the Jewish private soldiers and the Jewish generals alike. Major General O. O. Howard speaks of one of his Jewish staff officers as being "of the bravest and best," of another—killed at Chancellorsville—as being "a true friend and a brave officer." He highly praises two of his Jewish brigadier generals; finally, he uses these strong words: "Intrinsically, there are no more patriotic men to be found in the country than those who claim to be of Hebrew descent, and who served with me in parallel commands or more directly under my instructions."

Fourteen Jewish Confederate and Union families contributed, between them, fifty-one soldiers to the war—among these, a father and three sons; another, a father and four sons.

In the above article, I was not able to endorse the common reproach that the Jew is willing to feed upon a country but not to fight for it, because I did not know whether it was true or false. I supposed it to be true, but it is not allowable to endorse wandering maxims upon supposition—except when one is trying to make out a case. This slur upon the Jew cannot hold up its head in presence of the figures of the War Department. It has done its work, and done it long and faithfully, and with high approval: it ought to be pensioned off now, and retired from active service.